ANCHOR BOOKS

THE HUMAN ELEMENT

First published in Great Britain in 1994 by
ANCHOR BOOKS
1-2 Wainman Road, Woodston,
Peterborough, PE2 7BU

Foreword

Anchor Books is a small press, established in 1992, with the aim of promoting readable poetry to as wide an audience as possible.

We hope to establish an outlet for writers of poetry who may have struggled to see their work in print.

Following our request in the National Press, we were overwhelmed by the response. The poems presented here have been selected from many entries. Editing proved to be a difficult and daunting task and as the Editor, the final selection was mine.

The poems chosen represent a cross-section of styles and content. They have been sent from all over the country, written by young and old alike, united in the passion for writing poetry.

I trust this selection will delight and please the authors and all those who enjoy reading poetry.

Michelle Abbott
Editor

Contents

Family Values

What better sight there cannot be
Than to see a happy family,
With children walking hand in hand
To church and school are memories for me,
For marriage vows I understand
Were made to improve all mankind,
For in the end rewards will come
But now it seems for only some.
For patience, love and understanding
Is needed to keep a marriage working.
For all parents to love their children,
To always trust and pray for them, then,
They will look back with gratitude and pride.
So that way of life could abide
From one generation to generation.
Parents who do not love their children,
So sad, that's why they could go wrong
When feeling they do not belong.
So to always love and trust them
They will not want to let you down.
That is why I have always found,
That's what is needed in life today.
Although I fear it is lessening
The Family will always be, Bless them.

F Morris

The Dole Queue

I'm standing in the dole queue,
I'm signing on again,
The same old faces stare at me,
I'm with them once again.

I wake up in the morning,
Before the sun does rise,
I'm waiting for the post to come,
And then I go and hide.

The poverty around me,
It is so hard to bear,
No one ever notices you,
No one seems to care.

Pauline Clay

2

Creases

The wedge of the iron's bite
pushes apart the white wrinkles.
Now the seam is flat.

The flex tugs, catches on a toy-box;
she yanks it free, the chortles
and croaks of the steaming water
complaining for her.

Faces watch her from photo-frames;
she pauses to shrug at them.
They frown, foreheads rippled,
puzzling at the life around
that just will not come clean.

There's one gone his own way; another
closes her mind like gaol door.
Back to the sleeve and the creases.
These, she can manage.

Stephen Wade

Trouble

It's all those single mothers' fault causing a rise in crime
rearing young joy riders, who steal cars all the time.

They only have their mother, she some how lost the man,
hardly surprising, the young disregard society's plan.

They need a man about the house to keep them all in line,
with a father figure, everything would be fine.

Why, is she not at home tending to the needs,
Breeding latchkey children, sowing the seeds of

Trouble

> is, it's hard to be breadwinner, cleaner, cook
> carer and best friend. Time and energy expended
> prioritised given. In the end,
> poorly paid, part time work often the only choice
> with hardly any rights of powers, she needs a political voice.

Trouble
> with Politicians is, they are mostly men
> who have positions, money, power and then again
> leave their wives or mistresses to be single handed
> parents. This aside, no statistics prove those branded
> are single mothers' bundles of joy.

> So could it be a ploy, to bring back
> patriarchy, women and children knowing their place
> silenced, subdued . . .

> No

> Trouble.

Patricia Cattley

Brave Men in Tartan Kilts

We came down the glen with a thousand
men, who were ready to fight the war.
There were uncles and brothers, fathers
and sons, that's what we're down here for.
We took one look at the stonie crook and
we knew we had to cross, with sword
and shield and miles of field and the land
full of moss.

I said to my men - there's no turning back
and some will never return, if you want
to go - you better go now before the moon
shines on the burn.
So we marched on down with heads so
high and our hearts so brave.
We didn't know what was ahead and
we believed in the words we said.

A mile ahead we saw the enemy waving
their flags like hell, I said to my
men - blow those pipes and let's show
them our flag as well.
Face to face with swords raised we began
to shout our war cry, they came
in numbers and we fought hard
hundreds died and why.
Now the war is over and our heroes will
sleep in the land just below.
We will never forget those brave
men indeed and we'll fly our flag
so they will know.

William Limerick

Don't Leave Me

Don't leave me by the river bank
To see dead fish floating by
Crisp bags, bottles too, are there
And all I ask is *why*?

Don't leave me in the green meadow
To picnic in the litter,
Rubbish could be taken home
And leave the green much better.

Don't leave me standing in the street
To watch the dogs going by,
Owners careless of their dirt
Clear it up, they will not try.

Don't leave me paddling in the sea
Slime and rubbish to be seen,
The water that's polluted
You don't know where it's been.

Don't leave me to tell my Children
That filth is everywhere,
But take responsibility
And show them that we care.

Dorothy Mitchell

6

A Baby

A baby is a precious thing.
A baby is for life.
A baby needs love, and
Care, but most of all you
There, to take care of him.
So love and cherish,
This precious gift.
So lift him up,
Hold him tight then,
See him safely,
Through the night.

Wendy Cooper Gordon

Parents!

If They'd just let me out of my pushchair
I promise I'd not start to run.
I'd walk, holding hands with my sister,
But life would be so much more fun.

If They'd just lift me out of my playpen
I could then go and fetch my own toys,
And They could sit down with their feet up.
I promise I'd not make a noise.

If They'd just help me down from my highchair
I'd not throw my food on the floor.
I'd use a big spoon like my brother,
And I promise I'd not ask for more.

If They'd just leave me here in the bathtub
I'm sure I could soon find the soap.
Oh, why don't They understand children?
They just don't seem able to cope!

Marion Elliott

Me

I'm one of life's late developers
My childhood went by so fast,
The basic skill of growing up
Was something I failed to grasp.

Somehow I survived the first ten years
But my progress was very slow,
As a teenager I did little more
Than maintain the Status Quo.

By the time that I was twenty
I had scarcely outgrown my toys,
And it took me until I was thirty
To sort out the men from the boys.

At forty I made a great effort
To be all things to everyone,
But that proved an impossibility
And for me it wasn't much fun.

I'm slightly eccentric, often naive
And quite likely, this way I'll remain
While other folk struggle to cope with life
For me it's just one long game.

So here I am at fifty
Feeling my life's just begun,
The outside maybe past its sell by date
But inside, I'm still twenty one.

Sandra E Ronson

My Way

Please parents don't dictate
that can only lead to hate,
don't tell me what to do
I don't want to be like you
you can do and say what you like,
but this is still my life
even though I love you
and I know you love me too.
I have my own mind
and your ways are not mine,
so now please just let me choose
to do the things the way I please
maybe you won't like what I do
but that's not really up to you;
and even if we don't agree
that's no reason for us to be
arguing with each other constantly
for no one will win can't you see.

Eileen Kyte

10

Our Family

There's Tiddles our pussycat, Dizzy our dog
and Mummy and Daddy and me,
and Roger the rabbit and guinea pig Wee
and Tiny the hamster in our family,
at home where we live by the sea.
We're awfully happy to be
together in our family.

It would be so horrid if one Grown-up left us,
and broke up our nice family
of Roger and Tiny and Dizzy and Wee,
and Tiddles and Mummy and Daddy and me.
Without both my grown-ups I'd be
unhappy at home by the sea.
We must be a whole family!

Dorothy Headland

11

Elizabeth

Elizabeth, in your coach of gold,
Elizabeth, in your sparkling robe,
Elizabeth, with your smile so warm,
We'll pray for you, on that wonderful morn',
You're loveliness in your stately dress,
May your future be blessed with happiness,
You're our Queen at last, and we're proud of you,
   Your our own *Elizabeth*.

You'll have your Prince, so charming and gay,
He'll see you through, on that wonderful day,
As you walk down the aisle, all silver and gold,
You'll weave a memory, as in days of old,
The bells will ring, and the banners will fly,
Our hearts will sing, as we see you pass by,
In your crown of gold, you're a joy to behold,
   For your our own *Elizabeth*.

Ann Robb

12

Welcome Kellie

On Thursday, August twenty sixth
A baby girl was born,
Her entrance to this sad old world
Was greeted by the dawn.

Her face so pure, her skin so soft
Her hands and feet - perfection
Her thatch of hair like eiderdown
And peaches, her complexion.

She radiates such joy and love
A brand new life's begun,
She lies content within her cot
At peace with everyone.

As she grows, no doubt some obstacles
She'll meet along the way,
But with confidence, she'll master them
And common sense display.

My prayer for Kellie - simply
Love, affection - health, good friends
May she grow in perfect harmony
And human nature comprehend.

May her outlook be serene and calm
Her humour - sharp and witty,
May she think of others with good grace
Show compassion, love and pity.

So I dedicate this poem to her
She's two weeks old - so helpless,
Her birth has brought such happiness
A gift that's truly priceless.

Majorie C Edgar

13

The Rose

I was like that rose - proud and in full bloom.
The rush of colour on my face
would drain away all too soon
and leave a look of death in its place.

Surrounded by little buds and leaves
that protect me from the prickly thorn.
The ivy started creeping, through the bush it weaves
silently choking buds and leaving flesh all torn.

Its selfish journey once begun, would never ever end.
It crashed through, suckers ever seeking.
The trail of death, once caused, would never mend.
The heart of the rose had been seeked out, sadly it was choking.
The bush that was once a joy to be seen
had been drained by subtle strangulation.
With one last frantic grasp at life, I fell as if in dream.
The ivy trailed still further, no time for contemplation.

The petals fell, cascading down, from leaf to thorny stem.
The stabbing of each thorn that tore my flesh apart,
that whipped and tossed the buds and lacerating them,
did not hurt half as much as did my aching heart.

But one last breath was left in me
and I struggled hard just to survive . . .
My battered flesh lay bare, for all to see,
But I care not! I came through! *I am alive.*

Pam Handley

14

Conversation Poem

'Excuse me, do you know the way to the Town Hall?'
    'Where's a golf ball?'
'No do you know the way to the Town Hall?'
    'The Town Hall?'
    'Yes'
'The thing with the big clock on it?'
    'Yes'
'The thing the mayor visits?'
    'Yes'
'The thing they hold meetings in?'
    'Yes'
'The thing they . . . ?'
'Could you just tell me where it is!?'
'Oh!' 'It's just round the corner'
    'Thank you!'

Emma Watt (10)

The Bargain Hunter

Jeannie an' Maysie an' Maggie were chattin'
Doon near the end o' the street, yack-yacking'
Talk aboot everything under the sun,
Then back tae subject number one.

Mysie wis known as the bargain hunter.
Her tips were the best o' ony punter.
The best buys in toon - if a price wis *knocked-doon*
Mysie wis yin o' the first aroon'

Sae their lugs flappit up as she telt them the tale
O' the bargain buys at the latest sale.
An' Jeannie an' Maggie were ettlin' tae go,
First thing in the mornin' tae join the show.

Then roon' the corner came *soor-dook* Sam.
(The by-name gied tae Mysie's man)
An ill-favoured, gurly, thrawn wee deevil
That naebody ever kent tae be ceevil.

'Fine day!' said the wifies, as he drew near.
But he glumphed as his mooth drew in wi' a sneer,
An' Mysie sighed as the convoyed him hame,
An' thocht, 'Twas an ill day I took his name'

'Aye,' Maggie remarked, lookin' ower at the pair,
She didnae get much o' a bargain there!'

Margaret M Osoba

Lady Godiva

Women are angry!
We will fight back!

Bright Red spraycan letters
Sprawled across my marble base.

Do they think protest is new?
Or female anger original?

I protested bareback
eight hundred and thirty years ago

All it got me was immortality
and a very bad cold!

Irene Ison

Victims of Crime

Victims of crime
Their minds in distortion,
Families aroused
Never in suspicion.

The shock is traumatic
And often devastating,
Some need psychological help
When it's sexual abusing.

People often disbelieved
So charming they're described,
Being let down and betrayed
Knowing all the dreadful lies.

The questioning in a trial
And emotional stress and strain,
The heart ache of the victim
And families suffer the pain!

Sarah Whitehead

18

Anger

At everything,

Or at men?
>Stepfathers
>Fathers
>Boyfriends,
>Husbands
>Lovers
>Colleagues.

Years of abuse
Silently endured,

Until at last we break.

To be reviled by
Other men . . .
>Police
>Magistrates
>Judges.

We're only human
Members of the same race.

Minus, it seems
the human right to fight back.

Please God,
>let our daughters benefit
>let them have the silver lining
>because it may be too late for us.

Dedicated to Sara Thornton et al.

Jane Osmond

19

O Sister Mine

Two dainty hands, large eyes and smiling face,
A wistfulness, some charm and gentle grace,
A look of mischief and a fiery spark -
Upon a loved one's form these left their mark -
All in those childhood days.

Tempestuous moments and flash of passions bright
Consumed her energy through day and night.
In colours so bold and styles alarming
She made her way truly disarming -
Through all her teenage years.

Her loves in life were sadly shattered
When marriage bonds no longer mattered.
Her roles as wife and caring mother
Could be compared with any other -
These were her tearful times.

She journeyed homeward, back to native ground
With many thrilling pleasures newly-found,
And built a haven full of happy days,
Reorientating all her life and ways -
This was a joyous year.

A tumour struck a blow outrageous
Outwitting mind and heart courageous -
Against all odds she fought with might and main
And gradually her strength began to wane -
In those her numbered days.

Her ashen remains were scattered around
On the sloping side of some mountainous ground.
Alone with the birds and a few grazing sheep
She's only a memory for those who still weep -
But now she is really at peace.

Yvonne Watkin-Rees

Kinship

The family's for sharing, for comfort and care
In joy and in sorrow: just being there
Arguments yes, also laughter and tears
A place to return to: to quieten our fears.

Often widely dispersed but still bound by ties
Deeply and firmly, the root of our lives
When meeting together the years roll away
Memories reviving though deep they once lay.

Reaching out to new members to welcome them in
Brought there by marriage our as one of our kin,
Both are made welcome as part of the clan
And so it continues fulfilling life's plan.

Beatrice Smith

21

Untitled

There is much talk in nineteen ninety three about Families,
What are they and what do they mean?
Ask a dozen people and no doubt they would all give a different
answer

But, *Love is my meaning.*

I think from the very beginning there was man, woman and children
It had to be that way for survival.
Let us take the ideal: boy meets girl, they fall in love
They marry and raise their family; they all know each other
The good and bad, the security lies in being loved for what they are.

The reality is often different, one parent with child;
Pity the parent, no-one to share with,
The child, only half complete with only one set of relations,
What makes up the rest of me?

Man needs woman, and woman needs man, for life
Child needs father and mother, it is right.
Home is all of these things, and
Love is my meaning.

Cara Ross

22

Family Life

I've read a lot just lately on the perils of TV
The effect on children can, it said, be bad.
It stops you communicating, acting as a family,
So I switched it off and went and found their Dad.

So Sunday after tea was done and all the dishes dried
We gathered round the table everyone.
Monopoly, Strip Poker, Snakes and Ladders, were the cries
It doesn't matter what we play - we're having fun.

It took us half an hour or so to find a pack of cards
Dad dealt them around without a bit of fuss.
But someone sat on Bones the Butcher and the game just didn't
                                                        work
Their happy families seemed happier than us!

Dad was very pleased winning three games on the trot
But the kids thought he must really be a cheat.
And Mum could swear that somebody kept looking at her hand
And 'What's that card doing down there by your feet?'

So we had a go at Scrabble but someone couldn't spell
And Dad used lots of words we'd never heard.
Two were rather suspect, and one definitely rude
And a good old family argument occurred.

Monopoly was a failure as it nearly always is
Dad got hotels on Mayfair right away.
And when the kids went bankrupt and then got sent to jail
They hid the dice and said they wouldn't play.

So pack away the games Dad and switch the telly on
I can't stand all this trouble and the strife.
And we'll forget our squabbles watching Neighbours on the box
And away with this old thing called Family Life!

Margaret Daniels

23

Hidden Wealth

Some people think that I am poor
I have no wealth, as such
But what I have is so much more
No one could ever touch

My gold is in the sunshine,
That floats down from the sky
My silver is the falling rain
When the ground is dry

My jewels are my children
With four I have been blessed
They fill my heart, with so much love
And that's my treasure chest

My husband he is priceless
In fact he is unique
He's the only man, who ever could
Make my knees go weak

And when he says *I love you*
I feel just like a Queen
How rich I am, and yet you know
I haven't got a bean

Margaret Town

Family Values

The word keeps changing
But let us not change
For families together
Mean so much.
Take care of nature
We must do
For God gave us
All the beauty we do see,
For our children every one
To enjoy the simple things
Of Life.
Material things what
Are they
A mum and dad are
Everything,
So love each other
Every day
Pray for happy families.

Eileen Kisby

25

Uncles

Time was when Uncle Bill
Was the family clown at the house on the hill.
When Grandmama and suffering Granpapa
Entertained the family from wide and far.

Christmas was a special time
When all would come to sit down and dine.
Cousins, aunts and distant kin and especially Uncle Bill
Performing his best to provide a thrill.

But now, indeed, how times have changed
The family no longer gather as arranged.
Grandmama and grandpapa take to the skies
And spend Christmas abroad avoiding family ties.

Uncle Bill no longer entertains the masses
But takes himself off with various lasses.
So Emma and Jason must make do
With TV games and the video version of Dr Who

When their turn comes will they do the same
Or will they bring back the family game?
With Uncle Bill and the rest of the clan.
Alas! I doubt very much if they can.

For family feelings is something inbred
By the closeness of a family which is led
By the example of the older folk
Who know that life is not one big joke.

Iris Sheridan

The Sweet and Sour

A new one is born, born to join this wicked race
he's got to be strong, he's got to keep pace
to make his way yet stay alive
would be his only way to survive.

Young and vibrant, full of life
then married, now he's got a wife
one child, two and now three
he's no more young, he's no more free.

The good times have come and gone
life is going by quite fast
lots of things, now in the past
fifty, sixty, moving on,
the tide is moving in very strong.

He's old, he's grey
his bones they creek,
his breathing heavy,
his eyes; they seek,
he's gone through life sweet and sour
and nearer comes his last hour.

Kemi Olukotun

O' Man of the Street

Woods he lays his weary head,
Streets he trudges to keep warm.
Fragments of leavings he seeks.
Pride he has this humble man.

No begging for him,
Given food or money
He will take
Thank you he will say.

He cares not that
You do not speak,
In a world of his own he dwells,
Where men fear to tread.

Open to the elements.
Security exchanged for insecurity.
Known for the unknown.
Circumstances or choice?

No clinging for him
Possessions none.
No other human being,
He has himself.

In wonder we look
Feel respect and revere,
Clinging to our false security
Frightened to let go.

Truth may prevail
That we too are alone.

Sylvia Lewis

Auld Age

Fan ye start tae turn auld
That's fan ye start tae worry,
Ye dae yer best tae get aboot
Bit then ye canna, hurry.
Ye see the young ains' fleein' by
Wish ye could dae the same,
Creaky bones they let ye doon
Yer lucky tae git back hame.
Fan ye try tae clim' a hill
Yer chest it starts tae wheeze,
Afore ye git jist half whi up
Yer doon on bended knees.
Face turns grey an' pick-ed
Skin jist hings like rags,
Yer een the same auld colour
But underneath are bags,
Yet hair fas oot yer hauns the shak
Ye canna ate yer denner,
Tatties fa a oor the fleer
Wid sell ye for a tenner.
If ye laugh ye pee yersel
Canna hud in yer water,
Bowels they work overtime
Runs oot like ruddy batter.
Noo yer eyelids start tae droop
Yer eyebrows meet the gither,
The face is gaun through the change
Will hardly, bide the gither,
Though yer life's gaun through the stages
The human race an athing ages.

Elizabeth Fraser

29

Birthday Blues

Oh what a wonderful birthday
I woke to a wonderful thrill,
Oh what a wonderful birthday
All those long hours to fill.

Oh what a wonderful birthday
The forecasters hastened to say,
That for my very own birthday
Lots more snow was on the way.

So today you can say I am house bound
With snow inches deep at my door,
I can't get out and my friends can't get in
Who could ask for anything more.

I am sitting in front of that box thing
A drink in my hand as I view,
I'm toasting myself at the moment
The programme - I haven't a clue.

The dog comes and sits down beside me
He is wanting to go for a run,
I'm sorry, my love you're unlucky
A blizzard outside's just begun.

Oh what a wonderful birthday
Another whole year has rushed by,
At five years, a year is a lifetime
Now a lifetime is starting to fly.

Ah well, it's a wonderful birthday
I can remember those past with a smile,
I remember the love I've been given
To Birthdays - May they last a long while.

J Mortimer

Wheels

Stop, stop right where you are,
Who are you in that stolen car,
Driving around so very fast, for how long it lasts,
Your future is bleak, listen to me,
I am in a wheelchair, because of my *dare*,
Being so stupid and unaware,
Thinking of the fun, but not what was about to come.

Screaming friends are all that I heard,
As we turned and hit the curb,
What a mess, as I lay in that wreck,
Blood and guts, up to my neck,
Quick as a flash, it happened so fast,
No more walking, no not for me,
This is why I send out this plea,
I didn't want this to happen to me,
Who needs enemies, when you have friends,
Who will take you, right up to your end.

Edwina A Winrow

31

Poem for Patrick (March 17th 1993)

One hundred and twenty-eight years have passed
Since you married my great-great-grandmother.
She too was from Ireland; a couple of exiles
Thrown together in Preston's Back Canal Street:
Immigrant ghetto; Irishman's England,
Creators of cotton's wealth slaved side by side,
Spinning and weaving, grinding and stripping,
Back-breaking work forgotten in drink.
Irish whiskey - a trip to oblivion via
The homeland that forced you to leave,
Its green barren country a painful reminder
As Coketown's smog swept through your system.
The colds came more frequent,
The coughs never left you,
They couldn't cure you, pneumonia they knew
Killed many in those times; a strong lad of thirty
Worn into the ground by the capitalist's greed.
A wife and three children,
Your boy not yet talking,
Left with his uncle, as mother went home.
Unable, it seems, to live here without you,
She boarded the boat which was next Ireland bound.
But your one son survived; his boy my granddad,
Who I never knew - so all this I unearthed
Hunting through records of your humble existence,
And my pride at your blood in my veins overflows.

Peter Burns

Lunch Hour

It's been worth it -
eating my sandwiches out of sight
of Mr Jay's eagle eye.

Hello, my handsome man!
I love the great scroll that frames you.
I love the elegance
of your snow leopard cloak.
(Apologies to Animal Rights)

Why are you asking for my sympathy
with your melancholy gaze?
It is because the badge on your cap, says
I desire too much!

Unemployed, you could say
with time on your hands to write a poem
to my eyebrow.

She spoke very well for forty minutes -
Oil was a good medium, she said.
I can feel his hands - warm and soft to touch.

Mad rush back to the office
Mr Jay'll pinch my bum if I'm late.
He knows I'll not report him
if he overlooks not coming back, promptly
to those dreaded screens.

Benita Heaven

33

What We Need is a Woman's Army

What we need is a woman's army,
and the army, (or police force)
would know what you meant
by harassment, by rape, by put downs,
by phone calls, by harassment, by rape,
by put downs, by phone calls, by harassment.

You could ring up the army,
and they would understand,
because they have it too.

Would it be protection or revenge?
Would the men's army fight them
or stand back and let them go first?

It wouldn't work if we stabbed them all with kitchen knives,
. . . But it's a lovely thought.

Clare Davies

34

If I Were Dead

If I were dead
I'd be a ghoul,
And lurk at night down
In the hall.

Spiritually searching
through coats and hats,
I'd frighten off all
Mice and rats.

Cuckoo!
        Cuckoo!
The cuckoo clock,
It must be dawn
So now I must settle
And let life be born.

David Edwards (11)

My Darling Daughter

Too long you have trod a stony path,
Now, you never seem to laugh,
Your eyes have taken on a wary look,
As if you are trying to write a book.
My dearest daughter do not fret,
Your time will come for you yet.
So try to get over your heartache and loneliness,
Concentrate on Nature's loveliness.
Take heart and look around you,
At flowers which are starting to bloom,
There's a promise of spring in the petals,
The starting of love anew.
Take a fresh look at Nature,
Don't worry about the day,
Whether it's cold, rain, or snowing,
Nature will have her own way.
There is a God in heaven,
He looks after you still,
Lift up your heart to the sky above,
Be strong, have courage and joy fill your soul.

Elizabeth R Jordan

Holding Hands With Hannah

(To my granddaugher)

Reach out for my hand
Little one
And show me the world
Through new eyes.
Show me the hopes
of the future
With bright
And sunny skies.

Take hold of my hand
Little one
And drag me out
Of the past.
Make me forget
The depression
And gloom.
Show me hope at last.

Keep hold of my hand
Little one
So we can go forward together.
My generation, yours too,
You are the hope of the future.
The fate of the world
And all that is in it
Rests with you.

Barbara Harrison

Full Circle

My childhood memories are of poverty,
Poverty that is chilling to recall.
But I am looking back with adult eyes
That perceive my past childhood -
My orphaned state -
My endless search for the love I never found.
Nevertheless I grew
Both in body and in spirit,
I accepted who I was and where I was.
Because a child is accepting of what he cannot change.
Today's children too accept so much that is unacceptable,
Torn between conflicting loyalties,
Their lives disrupted by adult needs.
The child who is loved,
The child who is wanted.
The child that can say with childish glee,
'Watch me mummy - watch me dad,'
As some new skill has been learned,
This child is truly blessed.

Ivy M Goodley

Grandchildren

A knock at the door!
There they stand,
With broken toys and sticky hands.
In they step with their demands.
'I want,' 'I want,' is their war cry.
Not well behaved like in my day.
(Written by a Granddad with a short memory)

Michael J Hills

39

To My Grandson on His 1st Birthday

Thomas you're a treasure,
Thomas you're a pet,
You brought with you such pleasure,
Love and happiness.
It doesn't seem a year ago
I waited up all night,
To hear that you were in the world
Put everything to rights,
I changed my name to Grandma
On the 20th June.
God bless, I'll love you always,
Come and see me soon.

Maureen Stevens

In My View

I think poems that rhyme are best
'Cos, after all, they've stood the test.
I've tried my hand at *Modern Verse*,
And finished up with *Trash*, or worse!

It isn't everyone, you know,
Can write with rhythm and with flow,
And then contrive to entertain
Both Sage's thoughts, and Peasant's brain.

Free verse, you know, is really Prose,
And only dabbled in by those
Who feign some knowledge, most replete,
Or like to think they are Elite.

Of course, the fairer sex succeed
Far better than the *macho* breed,
Who simply juggle words around
Oblivious of how they sound.

The Laurel crown should surely, now,
Be placed upon a Female brow.
Unfortunate for men, it's true,
But lovely if it's me, or you!

Shirley Frances Winskill

41

The Yellow Brick Road

Waiting for it
That key in the door
Silently screaming
'Not again, no more!'

How will you be
Overly cheerful or angry at me?
What does it matter, the result is the same
Already she is broken and ragged with shame

Her soul has grown weary
She gave in from the start
Only in films
Can you find a new heart

The Road's been diverted
Dreams damaged beyond repair
Toys like her lie all broken
'Why, just why weren't you there?'

Deborah Gahan

My Giro

I hear the postman knocking, he's chapping on my door
I know he's got my giro, for I saw it hit the floor.
Every second Thursday, I look forward to this
Especially at Christmas time, for its better than a kiss.
For I've had letters of thanks, letters from cranks
And letters of joy from a girl to a boy.
Receipted bills and invitations
To go to the job centre, or visit relations.
And applications for situations
And past lovers declarations.
Letters with wedding snaps, to enlarge in,
Letters with faces scrawled in the margin
All written in paper of every hue.
The pink and the violet the white and the blue,
The chatty, the catty, the boring and adorning.
The cold and official, and the hearts out pouring,
The clever, the stupid, the short and the young.
The gypped and the printed, and some spelt wrong,
Some written in ink, and some written in biro,
But my favourite one is my fortnight's giro.

Donny Couper

43

The Doctors

When I went to the Doctors,
His name was Dr Chulse,
He stuck his fingers on my wrist,
And said I had no pulse.
He shouted through the speaker thing,
My my, oh my, oh my,
I think the chappie that's through 'ere
I think he's gonna die.
He said to me, 'My chappie, have you got one hundred pounds,
'Cos in a couple of days you'll be buried in the ground.'
I only went to see him, as I had the chicken pox,
But now I know in a week or so
I'll be buried in a box.

Alexander M Scott

Man all Alone

One man walks
Along a lonely highway
Following his step from all
the years before,
He does not notice that
The sun is rising
He only knows that his feet are sore.

Simon T D Black

Fear of Mr Scorgies' Belt

Fear of Mr Scorgies' belt, made me stutter as a child,
Words would tumble jump and rumble, better to be meek and mild.

Fear of Mr Scorgies' belt made my wee legs tremble cruel
As I ran, late yet again, oh mother didn't you know the rule?

Fear of Mr Scorgies' belt was there when joining CND
Man's indifference to fellow man was never to be part of me.

Fear of Mr Scorgies' belt made me brave and sometimes strong
My little son was gently shown the ways of right and wrong.

Fear of the belt was in us all, but how did Mr Scorgies feel?

Sandra Benedetti

46

Go Away Stephanie

Intrude into my thoughts - why don't you?

I am grey, drawn, dismal, violent.
In need of time, space, to neutralise . . .
To redress the balance, silently.

Suspend me in agar jelly, in a petri dish . . . with a lid.

Remove this cloud, this fallout acid rain.
Elevate, radiate me, enlighten-energise me.
Make me funny, make me laugh; heady with humour, wit: radiant.

Your eyes follow me, behind my eyes
- I see them as I saw them then;
Touching, secret, sensitive.

I take refuge in you.
As a beggar crawls up to the Church door after a lifetime of sin,
In search of salvation.
Where else could he go?

You are my life raft,
As torrents sweep me away from the banks of control.

And you have no idea.

Paul Frodsham

For I Am Still Asleep

Come softly to this bed of mine,
And lay yourself beside.
Touch gently, lest I soon awake,
In sleep I can't decide.

Awake, I could say yes . . . or no,
And you may be denied.
But sleeping I've no chance to speak,
The question's unreplied.

Then, cover me with kisses light,
My stirrings? . . . just a dream!
In slumber there is times a sigh,
All's not what it may seem.

So, let yourself be free to do,
The things that you desire.
I cannot hear, with eyes tight shut,
Your pounding heart of fire.

Look there! Another sleepy groan,
It happens in a doze.
I have not noticed you were here,
It's only you who knows!

Patricia Lee

The Dumb Girl

With difficulty
And a sorrow heart,
She tries to say
Mum.
But inside the word
Is deceiving her,
In despair, wanting
To let the world
Know, all the love
She got in her heart.
For the woman who
Gave her life and Love,
Crying in silence
And in pain.
Offer her hand to say
Let's go mum this is
A effort in vain.

G V Avanzato

Electrical Safety

Don't play with currents for a thrill,
    A hundred milliamps can kill,
Small batteries are safe, and why?
    'Cause our resistance is so high.
Mains wires we must never touch
    Because the power is so much.
And lightning with a million volts
    Can give some really nasty jolts.
Be careful not to go too far
    And just remember VIR.

D A Turner

Teenage Years

Now your teenage years have passed
And you sit down upon the grass,
Think about the fun you had
When you were just a little lad.

Having picnics in the park
Staying up after dark,
Playing football with your friends
Being mean to your brother Ben.

Your teenage years brought lots of joy
Discos parties having fun
Travelling round in the sun.

Your teenage years you never forget
Because when you're old! They were always the best.

Susan I Batchelor

Me

My values and feelings are me!
Who am I,
What am I,
Why am I,
Only I can see.

Just because I'm looking ruff,
Doesn't mean I am.

Just because I'm looking,
Old or young
Doesn't mean I am.

Just because I'm looking rich,
or poor,
Doesn't mean I am.

Just because I'm looking,
White, Black, Olive, Red,
Or Green,
Doesn't mean I am.

Just because I look like a lady
or a man
Doesn't mean I am.

I am what I am,
Not what others see.
Thank you for listening to me.

Anna Vrioni

52

A Special Person

My mum she is a special person,
As special as can be,
She's always there to comfort me,
If I fall and scrape my knee.
She's always there to help me,
If I am ever stuck,
She's always there to give me plenty of good luck.

My mum is very helpful,
And always there for me,
I know I can depend on her,
No matter what the problem may be,
She is so very special,
She means everything to me.
If ever I am feeling ill,
She pours me a cup of tea.

My mum is very loving and caring,
She is always prepared and very daring,
My mum is the best mum,
There ever could be,
I love her very much,
And she means the world to me.

Claire Freeman (10)

Mum's the Word

My very best chum
Is my dear old mum,
I think she is ever so sweet
She cooks and she sews
The holes in dad's toes
While his socks are still on his feet.

She cleans the house
And washes the clothes,
And clears up all our mess
It must be worth it I suppose
She still lives at our address.

When the telly's on
And mum's really gone,
On a juicy Saturday night play
Dad always comes in smelling of gin
And switches to Match of the Day.

On a weekend drive
Mum's up at five
To prepare us for the trip,
With dad at the wheel
We need more than a meal
It's a full survival kit.

It's thanks to my mum
And a bottle of rum,
That I am here today
Though my dad may regret
The first day we met
It was he who led mum astray.

P Hewitt

I Remember You

I'm thinking of you now
And I'm wishing you were near,
I often stop and think of you
When no-one else is here.

I think of all the things you said
And the way that we would laugh,
Never once did we think of
How quick the days would pass.

I'm thinking of the bygone days
When we would sit and talk,
I'm thinking of the quiet days
When all we did was walk.

I'm thinking of you still
I know I always will do
My truest and most loyal friend
I remember you.

Wanda Clark

My Ain Grandson

Wha' is this bairn that looks at me,
When I walk in the door?
He has a look aboot him,
I seem to have seen afore.

His hair is blonde, his eyes are blue,
He has a lovely smile.
I've seen this bairn afore, ye ken,
Though it seems to me a while.

This bairn he is an only child,
He has no sister or brither.
Where hae I seen this bairn afore?
I ken, he's like 'is mither.

His mither was my first born,
Five year ago and twenty-one.
This bairn I think I've seen afore -
He is my ain grandson.

Margaret C Robertson

Remember Mother

Always there when I needed you
to the very end.
You were more than just my mother,
You were my dearest friend.

I thank you for the happy years,
Your love and laughter before the tears
Your voice, your sayings your loving smile,
These are with me all the while.

You gave me love your whole life through,
and I'm so proud I belonged to you,
No-one knows my sorrows, there are few who see
Me weep, for I shed my tears in silence while
others are fast asleep.

So find a nice soft pillow God,
to rest her head upon,
Place my kiss upon her cheek,
and tell her who it's from.

Elaine Sweeney

Untitled

She ran the length of her life
with silent rage, and pain of an age.
displacing, unburdening, her bag of
miscellaneous emotions and a shattered
sense of self.

Death came a refuge, from this
her siege into the stillness of another
time, in the other place.

Joyce Spencer

Untitled

Am I alone?
Am I scared?
Am I beautiful?
Am I happy?
Am I satisfied?
Am I alive?
Am I useless?
Am I frigid?
I'm just hated,
By you, them and myself.

Zubeida

59

Someday

A Princess sat in her ivory tower
While the cream of her youth turned slowly sour,
Curdled and rancid but still she sat
Dressed in the fashion and wearing a hat.
She had her carrot juice for her lunch
And washed her long blonde hair,
She lowered it into the courtyard
And left it hanging there.
A Prince could easily climb it
She said as she watched it dry
It makes an adequate ladder
But none of the bastards will try.

M Windram Wheeler

The Lost Child

Where is my little one?
Is he far away?
Has he fled to Heaven?
I wouldn't let him stay
I had him ripped, I had him ripped away.

Did he feel the pain?
Did he wonder why?
I did love him, I did love him,
But he had to die
And I'm the reason, I'm the reason why.

Can I not forget him
Not forget him now?
He's dead and yet he never lived
Just a dream I would allow
Myself because it could not be
His face is one I'll never see,
It's forever lost, forever lost to me.

J C Earnshaw

The Beggar

He stands on the sidewalk
A man all alone,
A pitiful figure
Forsaken forlorn.

The crowds scuttle past him
No time for delay,
Just another old beggar
Not worth time of day.

But next time you pass him
Pay heed so I say,
Lest one day you too
Could stand as he does today.

Barbara Robinson

Walking Day

Tin bath's on the rug
So get yourselves in
Hurry up now no need for this din,
Two at a time
Let's see you shine
I want you all ready by half past nine.

Where is she now
I hear mam mutter
Oh my God! She says with a stutter
She's gutting a snig was all she could utter.

There's blood all over her walking day frock
Look out thinks me
Here comes the clock,
Right 'round my earhole
She lands me the clout
Was that me dad I heard sneaking out?

Down to the mission we all walk together
Like ducks with our mam at the end of her tether.
You're on a rope, not again thinks I
Looking up towards the sky
The minster's daughters are leading out
Like last year and next year again I've no doubt.

The sun's come out and the people throw money
Me dad's in the pub now isn't that funny,
Me mam is giving him withering looks
Well it was such a liberty he went and took
Messing me frock up on walking day.

J Chatterley

63

The Bag People

Piccadilly Gardens
That's where some of them live
By day.
Shop doorways and back alleys
By night.
Ten coats wide and a piece of string belt.
Ten bags each and a woolly hat.
Give them a wide berth.
Once I saw one,
Changin' his socks
They were clean socks
Someone must have scrubbed them.
Sometimes I wonder
Who they are.
Architects, tramps, mums and dads.
Skint or crazy?
Sometimes I wonder
If they were ever
Warm and welcome babies
Bundled into white blankets
In a smiling young woman's arms.

Carmen Walton

Elemental

Take belief in your hands
Cup and cradle it
And tend it on the flat and fertile earth
For all to share or marvel at,
This is yours
Enrobing and enlightening.

Breathe it through the air
Hear it in the tongues of men
A common parlance that can absorb,
And absolve
Or harness
Leaving unfettered
And so still free.

Yet fanned by the very air of truth
Those flames spitting on the testaments
Of its fondest allies,
Denuding of skin and hair
But not of faith
Its very saviours.

Bathe now in the waters
Staunch your wounds
They exist not,
Either here or in another place
Look out upon the path you laid
So firm
So easily trod

And sleep in calm.

David Learner

Life Goes on

Another day since she's been gone
Another hour that is lasting too long,
I keep on asking what went wrong
Life goes on without her.

I wash my dress just the same
I try my best to deny the pain,
But it keeps on coming back again
Life goes on without her.

She said she wanted me for me
She changed her mind, why I can't see,
Can't she see my love is free
Life goes on without her.

I tell myself I can be strong
And that I can carry on,
But this strength won't last long
Life goes on without her.

Another day turns to night
Another heart of faded light,
And still within my emotions fight
Life goes on.

Jack C Walters

66

My Best Friend

My best friend is really great
That is why she's my best mate,
She'll be my friend for ever and ever
We will always be together.

Jeci Payne

Remembrance Day

A tear for every petal,
Will be shed today,
For every piece of metal,
That ever found its way
Into the hearts of those we love,
Who are resting now above,
English, German, Dutch or French,
Were all the same when in the trench.
Husband, lover, son or friend,
They knew that it could be their end.
They died in such humility,
All war is just stupidity.

Patricia Ribbans

The Village That Cared

Little did they know, that fateful day
How big a part the roll of cloth would play
In shaping their lives in times to come,
An end for many, a chance for some.

The sickness began, first one then more
Death was soon knocking at the door
The village people met to talk,
They decided no longer could they walk
To neighbours scattered all around
No remedy for this plague was found.

The caring village stayed at home
Very soon their plight was known
People came to the well,
With food and clothes that they could sell
They left them there and when out of sight
The villagers came at dead of night.

This caring village remained locked and barred
Until the plague had left its scars
Death crept like mist, many felt its touch
The village people had suffered much
But it lived on and lives today
Many things it seems to say.

In our world now with pain and sorrow
Could we not begin as from tomorrow
To look at Eyam and learn
The way of life for which all yearn.

Vilma A Barton

Growing Old

Hold out my hand
To catch the time,
That runs through
My fingers and flies
To the ground.
Flies to the ground
The days like rain
Into crazy pools
Of uniform grey,
Dark as the clouds
The bore the rain
These days like rain
Will fall again.

Meena Ahluwalia

The Shopping Centre Louts

The precinct was once peaceful,
Not very long ago,
But now it has been ruined,
As the gangs refuse to go.

They shout and scream and drink and smoke,
These yobs, they do not care,
How can we expect to shop,
When there's violence everywhere.

I never enter the centre now,
For the louts, they make we wary,
They hurl abuse, as I walk by,
Which can be very scary.

The council just ignore complaints,
I do not think they care,
But when you live, next to the shops,
It really isn't fair.

I think that it is obvious,
That something must be done,
These groups, they should be dealt with,
For the sake of everyone.

I hope that this brief poem,
Helps you to understand,
The problems that these youths can bring,
And why they should be banned.

Fiona Bothwell

Going Somewhere

Little girl, where are you going?
Brown eyes full of trust are gazing
Up - inferring: *Do you love me?*
Yes of course! I answer smiling -
Then she holds my hand. Beguiling
Is her innocence - amazing!
Who will crush the fragile beauty;
Who will kill the starlight brightening
In that perfect little visage?
Someone will , some heartless prankster,
Who will guffaw like a gangster,
Then descend with talons tightening.
Little girl, where are you going?
Brown eyes dull with tears are gazing
Up - now mutely dumb however.
What can I do? How be clever?
Nothing I can say. I hug her -
No response this time - amazing?
Little girl has grown and married;
Fortunately someone caught her -
Coaxed her back to love and laughter -
Showed her how to face the devil -
Turned her face to higher level -
Yes - she could have been my daughter!

Dulcie Sharland

My Wife and I

The door flies open, a vase falls with a smash,
one mis-timed step, and I go down with a crash.
I shout out. 'Wife. where's my bleeding tea?'
Same reply. 'In the dog, where it ought to be.'
So it's two steps forward, and one step back,
as my head hits the rolling pin, with a loud crack.

Into the bedroom, I crawl on all fours,
to the musical score of loud slamming doors.
The housekeeping money is next on the list,
before I can answer, my mouth's holding a fist.
Still my loving wife, I could never hope to leave,
as I swing 'round the room, attached to my sleeve.

The next thing I know, I've landed on the old bed,
with the hot water bottle wrapped around my head.
My blackened eyes are still shining with love,
for a lump I still call my little turtle dove.
But when tomorrow comes, it will all start again,
when it's down to my local to drink away the pain.

And so my family life will always remain the same,
with everything I stand for, going right down the drain.
Behind the front door, I know she'll be waiting for me,
holding the frying pan, while the dog scoffs my tea.
This time I'm crafty, the back door lets me in,
but something hits me, and I end up sat in the bin.

Michael Yarwood

73

Child of Divorce

They buy me things, and that is very nice.
I like the things they give me, oh, I do.
They tell me that they've fallen out of love,
And then they say, 'Oh, but we still love you.'
My dad has grown to love somebody else.
I think my mother may have done that too.
So, if they've changed so much, how do I know
They won't fall out of love like that with me,
And want somebody else's little girl?
I'm Wednesday's child, I'm feeling full of woe.

K Farley

Time on His Hands

As apprentice boy he served his time
To qualify for a place on the assembly line
Where the money was good if reactions were quick
'Twas a race against time, so fast went the tick
But the body moves slower, as the time turns to years
He looks more at the clock, which confirms all his fears
The pace he can't keep, he will have to retire
And spend the rest of his life near his old coal fire
Where time it won't matter, so isn't it funny
That his gift on retirement was a clock, not the money.

Carol Ann Field

Aiming for the Sky

I can fly
if you let me.

I can fly . . .
I don't know
how high . . .
but I'll never know
till I try.

But you'll only let me fly
if I have to
- if you go
or die.

You'll be sad
not to be around
- to see me plummet
from on high.

But you'll be wrong.
And I'll sing you a haunting song
as I soar to the top of the sky.

Julie Callan

In Answer to Your Question

Yes, I'm still three paces behind
your father, he's quicker than me
at finding the way ahead, the geography,
he keeps the map in his mind.

No hang-up from our Arab life,
I carry no pot on my head,
nor do I share his table, his bed
or his thoughts with another wife.

But trekking together as we have done
through many times and seasons
we need our space, we know our reasons.
We must not crowd the winter sun

but give our shadows room to grow.
And while he navigates the path
I'm free to explore the undergrowth.
These are some things that you should know.

Pamela Wilkie

The Perils of the Self Employed

My husband said, 'I guess this chair will suit 'er.'
When he helped me organise my home computer.
But that wooden dining chair gave me such gyp -
So painful for my poor arthritic hip.
I cried in pain at night time in my bed.
'She's really peeved with work,' my husband said.
One day I spoke to Bob (the man next door);
He said, 'I've just the thing you're looking for -
I've found an office chair for you to test,
Its padded seat will give your hip a rest.'
Dear reader, it was ecstasy to see
A twizzly, cushioned chair just right for me:
And oh, what comfort! when I sat upon it,
It was the inspiration for this sonnet!

Marion Whiting

The Same Again Next Year

Big brown eyes
Covered with flies
And that protruding tummy,
Does it matter if it's Jane or Suny?
Clutching a bowl,
As big as their head
Scratching at the bottom
With fear and dread,
Looking inside for a grain or two
Standing or sitting in an endless queue,
With stick like legs
They are forced to beg,
No mum, no dad,
That they can claim,
The only friend they want is rain,
It may come in a year or two,
But in the meantime
What can they do,
Let us show a little pity,
All that live in town or city.

Gertrude Worrall

Grey

An old grey lady
In the coffee shop
In an old grey coat,
In an old grey hat
Eating a doughnut.

Daintily
Slicing it up
Carefully,
Scraping up
Every grain
Of sugar
With a white plastic knife.

Is it really so good?
Do you relish it so?
Or could it just be
That it makes time go slow
In your little grey life
To slice up your doughnut
With your white plastic knife.

Ann McCrory

For J Who Said I Smelt of Mothballs - With Love

As insulator
Against the Arch-Hater
To obscure the truth,
Of the grave I soothe
Whatever befalls
My days with mothballs?

Paper, ink
And what I think
Are likely to stink
But are no doubt clouded,
Scented and shrouded
With artful invention.
A fine intuition
For most of us here
On earth J dear
And for those whose homes
Are desperate poems.

As for me my verse
Can sometimes smell worse
Than a prettified hearse . . .

Jane Freeman

81

Ode to Landy

Six years ago she joined our band,
Diploma, badge and tape in hand,
To girth the ladies of proportions,
With corsetry - oh those contortions!

In private cubicle she fitted,
Mesdames - as in and out she flitted,
To find the only one for them,
So they would oft' return again.

They all learnt to love our Landy,
The answers to their problems Handy,
And as the time wore on apace,
All warmed to her endearing face.

To us - the staff - some lively tales,
She told at coffee break - and wails
Of laughter rang throughout
As Landy's anecdotes did spout.

But now, alas, we are to lose her,
New colleagues she will soon encounter,
Her cheery word will pass the day,
With other *girls* at work and play.

No longer will we hear *my pleasure*,
As Landy speaks of her endeavour,
And never will there be a day,
When we forget her pleasing way.

We wish her luck in her new life,
And hope it will be free of strife,
With fondest love we will recall,
Her six full years among us all.

Joyce Watson

Untitled

I drink from this cup of venom
brimming forth with warm beer and friendly chatter.
You pirouette charmingly before me
but I see you -
transparent
and I, wooden.
I am your tree,
Roots dance behind my eyes
green shoots break from fingers and toes.
And so snugly, I fit in this chair,
Smiling, quite desperately.
Chanting of my solitude.
I am your little monster,
rooted here,
watching your so familiar act.
I am your seed.

Sarah Nicholson

The First Steps

Nestled in sweet sweet milk
And soft white robes
of kisses,
Cuddled in sleepless twilights
And whispering nights of musical hushes
Rocked in a cradle of so many dreams,
My future.
Now standing, so proud, so excited
With little white socks and satchel
Copper hair shining, face expecting
Holding my hand that was so protecting
Breaking free and running with glee,
The first steps that will take her
Away from me.

Karen A Neville

Untitled

Raw emotional energy
I dare not release
churns, bursting inside my head,
excitement, energy, power
contained,
too little time to unfold it neatly
and so I jump from one high to the next
careful to avoid the chasm between,
give me time and vision before I fall.

Christine Rodgers

A Sonnet

Proof by demonstration; that was the aim.
Proof, if not to them, at least to me.
You learn the rules, and then you play their game
To emerge the victor; smug. You've made them see.
Anapests and iambs: thus to expose
These self-appointed arbiters of art.
Grand masters of illusion who suppose
Their fine pretensions set them in a world apart.
But now suspicion looms. Who lives the lie?
Am I just a fool to call them fools?
An eagle: does she know, or simply fly?
Floating, soaring, oblivious to the rules.
Perhaps I try too hard. Perhaps my mind,
Addled by analysis, has made me blind.

Peter B Hayward

Aloneness

It would be nice to have one human soul
        upon whom one could depend;
a kind, compassionate soul to share
        pain, and joy of living as a friend;
whose words not only offer promises
        of better quality of life,
but whose temperament would cope
        with any personal strife;
we cannot all be perfect,
        each has a cross to bear;
we need an honest friend whose sense of fun and
        comprehension nothing could impair.
Soul to soul companionship means much
        as decades come and go;
communication with an honest friend
        helps embers of *aloneness* to really glow!

R B E Scott

87

The Secret

I was feeling sad and gloomy
on a cloudy day in May.
I answered the telephone,
and I heard my daughter say.

'Would you like to hear a secret,'
her voice was light and gay.
The news she had to tell me
banished all my gloom away.

'I'm going to have a baby,'
I heard my daughter say.
Then the sun came out to celebrate
that day in early May.

Dorothy Dawson

Missing Daddy

Memories of being your little girl,
Who tagged along with you.
Memories of growing to teenage years,
Gone so quickly, seemed so few.
Memories of being a wife and mum,
and making you a granddad.
Memories to make me very happy,
and sometimes very sad.
Memories are all that's left now,
For your life came to an end.
Memories of my precious dad,
Father, mentor and dearest friend!

Gloria Birch

Bullies

There are several kinds of bullies
with that you must agree.
There are fat ones, and thin ones
And ones like you and me.
There are brother ones and sister ones
And parent ones as well.
But the most surprising ones of all . . .
And I know they'll *disagree*
Are teacher ones, headmaster ones
The ones with a degree!

Claire Stevens

My Constant Friend

The only companion
I have is my dog
He was seven and six pence so he costs
Quite a bob
But he's given me pleasure
All over the years,
When he's doing wrong he perks up his ears
He listens to the voice saying, 'Obey,'
With his head on his paws
He looks my way,
His sorrowful eyes that shine so bright
I feel I could cuddle this bundle so tight.
His fur's patched in places
And he wobbles around
He's getting quite old but he's still quite sound
I wouldn't part with my constant friend
He's my life and my love right till the end.

S Stuart

Talk to Me

A bottle raised to the lips,
A spirit pours into the bottle.
It drains the feelings,
Of so many people.
It drains the love,
Of so many people.
It steals the lives,
Of so many people.
Talk to me,
Said so many people.

Natasha Reidy

Some People

People with passion,
A fire in their eyes,
A belief in what they feel,
Free from soul destroying lies.

People with compassion,
Ambition and drive,
Pure love in their heart,
A love for all alive.

People who accept,
And have a will to live,
People who see good in bad,
And are always ready to give.

These are the people,
Who live a life well,
Their's is the glory,
The freedom from hell.

Susan Aiton

Walk on

See old Meg plod up the hill,
Along the stony track,
The fields lie in a quivering haze
Across her mottled back.

Old Meg, take the turning left,
Whoa down, and now walk on,
Only you are left to drive,
Now Bob and Trix have gone.

Old Meg's ears are twitching
At the farmer's shout,
Scamp, the dog, her enemy
Is somewhere near about.

Meg gives an angry snort
And proudly shakes her head,
Half her life she wished that Scamp,
The wretched dog, were dead.

So what if Farmer Patchet
Allowed his dog to roam,
Old Meg's pace is quickening
Now she's nearly home.

The cottage chimney's smoking,
The family are at tea,
And winding up the country road,
There's only Meg and me.

The sun is dipping westwards,
The light has nearly gone,
Old Meg gives a friendly neigh
As I say, 'Walk on.'

Ann Rutherford

94

Audience Participation
Marienkirche - Tübigen July 28th 1984

He came down amongst us
from the loft above, to conduct
our song in harmony.
Was the clarity because
pillars of sound
arched upwards,
curving into air,
and that this was new,
once only, for us?
Scattered now, we have the music;
word written for a memory,
and to rehearse.

Rosemary A Hector

A Step Forward

T Travellers along the same road,
H Harmony helps sharing the load.
E Everyone involved, should be the theme.

Y Young people must be part of the team,
O Older people, must the young, involve.
U Unity, or community voice will dissolve.
N Numerous talents we should explore,
G Group involvement we cannot deplore.

A Adolescence is no interlude,
D Developing skills we must not preclude.
U Unity need not be uniformity,
L Liaison is a must, though not conformity.
T Trust is the binding factor!

J Henderson Lightbody

To Mirander (Next Door)

Miranda you're mean.
You 'oller and scream.
You've got a kind mum and dad.

Miranda you're thin
with no hairs on your skin.
You've got a kind mum and dad.

Miranda what's wrong.
Burst into song.
You've got a kind mum and dad.

With nose red and titchy
and ears like a pixie
it all so obviously shows
that after this labour
I'm just a neighbour.
Mum and dad think you're a beautiful rose.

Patricia Freestone

After Seeing Edward Thomas's Memorial Stone

I stayed because the quietness was still and fresh -
Because you had walked this way many times -
Where all your words were surveyed - enveloped from
those back days
and instilled into the crevices where I now stand today.
Each violet and cowslip patch were here before - where you
had perhaps noticed too
Their gentle fragrance amid the hawthorn bush and shadowed
layers of jaded grass -
And here too the sun bows before this oval stone
Erected to the memory of you -
I stand in amazement - transfixed - to look upon this view
That you had looked upon so many years before
The black despairing war
Had lured you away -
I understand now
Your need - Your solitude -
Your love for all things fresh and pure -
Your secret, silent thoughts -
Where only the wind had touched your dreams -
And the call of the cuckoo summoned you home -
And the sound of the war
Had called you to your *Death*.

Barbara Kelsey

The Greatest Champ Muhammed Ali

Oh what entertainment what a good night
The time I went to see,
The greatest man ever fight
He's got the cutest shuffle
Anyone could wish to see,
The greatest fighter
In the world Muhammed Ali.
No man could ever beat him
No man could put him down
No matter how they hit him
He would never hit the ground,
You could never see a mark on him
He always looked so pretty
But then of course,
He was the champ Muhammed Ali.
Oh what entertainment what a good night
The time I went to see
The greatest man ever fight
But just look at his footwork,
And where's his famous sting
What is it that's gone wrong for him
Tonight in the ring,
What a disappointment
This time for us to see
He lost the fight,
The greatest champ Muhammed Ali.

Marjorie Arnett

I Did Not Seize Enough

I did not seize enough of careless fun
For I believed the chance would come again.
I did not know that life would take and stun
All that I was with suffering and pain.
My adult life seemed only just begun
I felt that I was strong and brave and sane.

The doctor's hint that I might not be sane.
They do not know my appetite for fun,
The love of life, which folds away with pain
The quick, light mind that all my symptoms stun.
They do not know, I long to live again
The adult life I'd only just begun.

As I lie, still and silent, I've begun
To think the doctors are not really sane.
Or, if they are, they must be having fun
Playing at God, while I lie here in pain.
In hospitals, I've found they seem to stun
The sick with tests, to make them worse again.

The thoughts churn in my head and churn again.
It's not as if the stress had just begun.
For years I wondered who was really sane.
Though doctors blamed depression I had fun,
Was I then manic? And the sense of pain
Delusion? Stress and awful tiredness stun.

But so dies pity. Other's hurt did stun
My courage once. It made me weak again.
I did not know I had a need of fun,
A right to ask for help. I'm still quite sane,
Much wiser than I was, for I've begun
To understand that I can't hold all pain.

Each day the *news* another source of pain.
The things you cannot help. It's meant to stun
To grief and silence. Passive once again
We will forget the good things we've begun.
We'll think that hope is hardly for the sane
And feel sad guilt in every bit of fun.

Then take the fun, you have your share of pain
Never again will light and beauty stun
The life begun when all the world seemed sane.

Phillipa Roberts

101

Of Lame Ducks

'You must be crazy!' exclaimed my friend, Paul,
When I said that young Jill, up at The Hall,
Was the one for me . . . that I meant it, too.
'Ah well,' said Paul, 'it figures, knowing you;
A sucker for lame ducks you've always been.'
'And what,' I asked, 'is that supposed to mean?'
'Oh, come off it, chum,' replied Paul, 'you know
Exactly what it means, you're not that slow!
It means, you've chosen Jill because you feel,
When it comes to looks, she's had a raw deal;
And so, you've added her to your long list
Of lame ducks which you never could resist;
And dearly they've cost you, more oft' than not!
What's more, in most cases, no thanks you've got
From suchlike, for of them taking pity.
Oh, I know it's got naught to do with me . . .
But a long way back we two go, and so
I can't just stand by and say naught, you know,
While you let yourself be ruled, overruled
By pity; and by it, too, conned and fooled
Into you letting your heart rule your head . . .
Knowing how oft' to disaster that's led!
I'd not be seen out with that weirdo, Jill!
Anyway, what about Jill's sister, Lill?
Young, sweet and lovely . . . a rare 'un is she;
And anyone, with half an eye, can see
That she's gone on you . . . yet, you've chosen Jill!

Can't understand you . . . guess I never will.'
'Look, Paul, I know that you mean well,' said I,
'But Jill is still the one for me; for my
Heart tells me: that - plain, lame duck though she be -
Love will change her into a great beauty.'
'From a duck to a swan?' said Paul, and laughed,
'Jill become a beauty! Don't talk so daft.'
But I'd the last laugh, Paul had to agree,
When Jill became a champion collie!

Ward Handforth-Holroyd